This booklet is a
lovely-named pl

Who lives in Tittymouse Wood, Twitty Fee and Twizzlefoot Bridge?

What happens to the ladies of South Woodham Ferrers, Hatfield Broad Oak and Stansted Mountfitchet?

What rhymes with Steeple Bumpstead, Shellow Bowells, Wendens Ambo and Tolleshunt d'Arcy?

These, and a hundred more posers, can all be solved if you buy this little book, and you'll be helping EWAG to support some of the less fortunate Essex girls and women, at the same time.

GC

Published by:

Essex Women's Advisory Group

Copyright:

© Essex Women's Advisory Group (EWAG), 2010

First printed and bound in the UK in 2010 by
Alphaprint (Colchester) Limited
Colchester, Essex CO1 2LY

Essex Girls'
Limericks

Edited by

George Courtauld
Chairman
Essex Women's Advisory Group

A young lady from **Essex** once said,
"All they want is to get me to bed;
(It's my long, blonde hair,
And provocative stare),
But I'd rather a wedding instead."

DC

From **Dagenham** bare footed came Sandie,
Representing on TV, Royaume-Uni;
The song she had to sing,
Was Puppet on a String,
Her hit parade topper number 3!

DF

Who lived in **Tittymouse Wood,**
Who was clever, and sweet, and good;
And had long blonde hair,
And an innocent air?
An Essex girl - Red Riding Hood!

GC

A highwayman rode out from **Stebbing,**
Through **Barnston** and then **Margaretting;**
He thought he was clear,
But lost all his gear,
To a buxom young lassie from **Epping.**

NC

It's so windy down in **Canewdon,**
That most ladies with hats keep 'em glued on;
But a Professor of Arts,
Yelled "what do you do with your farts?"
I'm afraid she was rather a lewd'n.

NC/GC

The lady from **Ardleigh** who sold gravel and stone,
Got very excited if they dug up a bone;
One day at the quarry,
She said, "I'm so sorry,
But I think you have buried my phone!"

VI

There was an old widow from **Toosy***,
Who took up with Death, as his floozy;
When friends expressed doubt.
She said: "Time's running out.
And at my age, you cannot be choosy."

He's cheerless and dark, as they say,
With attending disasters all day;
But he's a quite a nice bloke.
Underneath that black cloak,
Though his scythe tends to get in the way."

(* the local name for St. Osyth)

MN

A merry young maiden from **Barking,**
Was accused by a warden of larking;
And **Mucking** about,
Thus causing a rout,
And worse, of incompetent parking!

GC

On the coast, where abides the **East Saxon**,
The weather alarm is a claxon;
To tell all the fellers
To get their umbrellas,
And the ladies to button their macs on.

GC

An old lady from **Westcliff-on-Sea**,
Had cockles each day for her tea;
She caught them each morning,
When others were yawning,
So they were not only fresh, but buckshee.

DG

A lady who lived in **Bicknacre**,
Was so rude that no fellow would take her;
So she moved to **Great Oakley**,
To seek a man locally,
A pacifist saint or a Quaker.

GRG

Benfleet Betty was tall for her age,
At a time when 'petite' was the rage;
From stooping so low,
She excelled at limbo,
And starred on a Las Vegas stage.

DG

At **Layer Marney**, (the house with the gate),
They entertained Henry Mark VIII;
For his pad at **New Hall**,
Was then scarce built at all,
And for Essex girls Hal couldn't wait!

GRG

Some women of **Braintree** and **Witham**,
Wear outfits so tight they don't fit 'em;
Going south of the county,
It's viewed as a bounty,
In **Frinton**, they don't know what's hit 'em.

MN

There was an old lady of **Feering,**
Whose diminishing eyesight made peering;
A constant requirement,
Which unfortunately meant,
That everyone thought she was leering.

ME

An amateur witch from **Mount Bures**,
Had an out-of-date book on folk cures;
She poisoned the squire,
And much of the choir,
On a potion of pony manures.

GC

but

A dowager duchess from **Bures**,
Was a mug for alternative cures;
She chewed garlic for wrinkling,
Raw onion for tinkling,
Which all but destroyed her allures.

TR-S

Miss Blogg was a dishonest cleaner,
Who worked at the **Burnham Marina**;
Like it or not,
She stole an 80 foot yacht,
And no-one has since ever seen her.

JH-W

A sailor from **Walton Backwater,**
Had a very unseaworthy daughter;
She was frequently seen,
Her face **Matching Green**,
As they paddled along the **Blackwater.**

GRG

A milkmaid from **Chadwell St. Mary,**
Decided her legs were too hairy;
So she scrubbed them with milk,
'til her skin was like silk,
And now she's the belle of the dairy.

PC

A nervous young girl gave a squeal, she,
Said 'that horrid man's eyes are all steely;
His lecherous stare,
Strips me totally bare,
Oh, take me back home to **Chignal Smealey."**

GC

I met a fair cook, the prettiest seen,
Walking one day, towards **Bumbles Green**;
I gave her, to please her,
A new lemon squeezer,
Some millet, a skillet and a small soup tureen.

GC

The boobs of our Sharon were plastic,
Her figure was really fantastic;
But in **Frinton** one day,
She melted away,
Apart from her knicker elastic.

DF

A **Canvey** girl, famed for her curves,
Found when driving, her car did odd swerves;
Leaning one way or t'other,
The steering she'd smother.
Her passengers needed strong nerves.

DG

When visiting **Clacton** with friends,
Young Elaine enjoyed setting trends;
Hair and clothes drew attention,
But she loved the reception,
It's being ignored that offends.

DG

A disgusting old person from **Clavering,**
At the sight of a nice girl starts slavering;
In **Steeple Bumpstead,**
Politely, instead,
They bow at the girls they are favouring.

GC

There was a young lady from **Nazing,**
Whose talents were truly amazing;
She tamed lions, flew 'planes,
Modelled clothes and cleared drains,
She could even install double glazing.

PC

A **Colchester** cutie called Lou,
Made a hash of her acting debut;
As Queen of the Nile,
Although she had style,
She'd forgotten her Elvis tattoo.

DG

On the island that's called **Havengore,**
She lived by the cockleshell shore;
In a little chalet,
Which she left every day,
With a damp bathing suit on the floor.

GC

A chap who lived in **Coldharbour,**
Worked frantically hard as a barber;
So his wife - name of Maisie,
And uncommonly lazy,
Could idle her time in an arbour.

GC

There was an old girl from **Cold Norton,**
Whose name was Grizelda Frogmorton;
This venerable bint,
Had a formidable squint,
And a large purple nose with a wart on.

GC

A well bred girl from **Finchingfield,**
Dreams of marriage to a chap well healed;
She shows her good breeding,
In a bed where she's weeding,
She bends over, but nothing is revealed.

DC

At the ball, to and fro, to and fro,
Waltzed a lady from **Wendens Ambo;**
The end of her joy
Was a hobbledehoy,
Who trod on the tip of her toe.

GC

Our post-girl in **Burnham on Crouch,**
Conveys all her post in a pouch;
She is pretty and keen,
So ardently seen,
By the sailors who sail on the **Crouch**.

CC

An affable lady from **Cressing,**
Had a hobby of public undressing;
Though greatly admired,
She was not as desired,
As a far fatter lady from **Messing.**

GC

A wife, from **Ramsden Bellhouse,**
With anger, berated her spouse;
"That man fondled my bum!
But you did nothing, by gum!
Do you think you're a man, or a mouse?"

GC

A woman from **Cuckingstool End,**
Has a big brown baboon as a friend;
Her aunt from **High Garret,**
Is fond of a parrot.
This foursome plays bridge in **Southend.**

GC

West Bergholt's a charming delight,
Tho' Rosie once caused quite a fright;
By riding along,
In pink bra and thong.
The drivers all stopped at the sight.

NC

A lady from **Dagenham** called Sue,
Wore white stilettos to **Colchester** Zoo;
Whilst feeding a chimp,
Her arms went all limp,
And feeding no more she could do.

VI

A lady from **Dedham** named Peg,
Went to work one day on an egg;
But this, I fear,
Was a cracked idea,
As she fell off and fractured her leg!

DF

A London-bound girl from **Earls Colne**,
Incessantly talked on her 'phone;
Until a commuter,
Threatened to shoot her,
And flatten her 'phone with a stone.

GC

An infantile lady from **Fobbing,**
Was often heard sighing and a–sobbing;
She cried out her eyes,
For the unhappy demise,
Of that unfortunate birdie, Cock Robin.

GC

A dancer from **Beaumont-cum-Moze,**
Grew a number of warts on her toes;
She said "my career,
Is over, I fear,
But it's better than being on my nose."

PC

A charming young miss from **Gay Bowers,**
Liked dancing besprinkled with flowers;
She was nimble and neat,
Looked winsome and sweet,
When skipping midst soft summer showers

GC

There was a fiancé from **Boreham,**
Who'd two beauties but nowhere to store 'em,
When a men's choir from **Harwich,**
Performed at her marriage,
They sang "Oh come, let us adore 'em"

GRG

A little old lady from **Grays,**
Went out for a swim wearing stays;
She shouldn't have ought'er,
They shrank in the water,
And she went back to **Grays** in a daze.

GC

A lady from **Stansted Mountfitchet,**
Had a remarkable bust – she could twitch it;
"For adjustment", she said,
"I stand on my head,
That's always the best way to hitch it."

GC

"I'm in terrible need of a penny!"
Cried a frantic old girl from **Great Henny;**
"I've got tenners a-plenty,
And even a twenty,
But of pennies - I haven't got any!"

GC

Two Birds from **Chigwell**, Sharon and Tracey,
Went to Lakeside to buy something 'racey';
One wanted leather,
The other feather,
But they both ended up with black and lacey.

VI

A hairy old girl from **Great Leighs,**
Once thought she would like to keep bees;
But she cried, "As I feared!
They've got into my beard,
I'd be much better off growing peas."

JB

A lady from **Clacton-on-Sea,**
Was as plucky as plucky could be;
When her husband cried "Go!
'Cos I fancy your bro,"
She shot him three times in the knee.

PC

This beautiful lass from **Great Totham,**
Had her love's name tattooed on her bottom;
But it went round a bend,
Rather too near **Southend,**
Her father found out and shot 'em.

GRG

Another young lady from **Totham,**
(Whether **Little** or **Great**, I've forgotten);
Had a big spot,
Upon her fair bot,
And it hurt her to sit, something rotten.

JB

A skinny young girl from **Great Yeldham,**
Botoxed her small boobs, which then swelled 'em;
So together she tied,
Two sacks side by side,
And in that receptacle held 'em.

GC

A well-brought up girl from **Hare Green,**
Had a mind that was utterly clean;
So she smiled when a bloke,
Made a really crude joke,
Not knowing it was rude and obscene.

GC

A new lady vicar from **Birch,**
Decided to cheer up the church;
So she spiced up the wine,
'Til it tasted divine,
then rolled down the aisle with a lurch.

PC

A girl from the **Island of Frogs,**
Wore a huge pair of waterproof clogs;
Some heavy tweed skirts,
Two coats and four shirts,
(It's a cold and damp place, full of fogs).

GC

They cried: "what a funny address!"
To a girl from the **Isle of Foulness;**
She answered quite smugly,
"I'm neither **Mucking** nor **Ugley,**
Nor go **Messing** about when I dress."

GC

There was a young girl of **Great Bromley,**
Who everyone thought was most comely;
Except for her dancing,
All giggling and glancing,
And wriggling uncouthly and rumly.

GC

A tourist to **Kirby-le-Soken,**
Was, alas, not very well spoken;
She drove folk round the bend,
"Cos I came frum Sarfend,
Where they talks like I gotta be jokin."

GRG

A virtuous maiden from **Bocking,**
Thought all men's intentions were shocking;
So they wouldn't go far,
She put snakes in her bra,
And a fence round the top of each stocking.

GC

A lady from **South Benfleet,**
Discovered her boyfriend had smelly feet;
He went to the docs,
Who gave him new socks,
She now hopes there will be no repeat!

VI

When in **Leigh-on-Sea**, Becky said,
"The ozone has gone to my head";
But as Becky was boozing,
And gambling (and losing),
She may have been slightly misled.

DG

Six pretty young girls from **Mill Green,**
Decided to make quite a scene;
They pranced round the park,
Utterly Stark,
The result was supremely obscene.

PG

There's a really weird cow-girl from **Nazing**
Whose hobby is truly amazing;
She frequently ventures,
To put on <u>huge</u> dentures,
And browse with her herd in their grazing.

GC

An unfortunate girl from **Great Leighs,**
Was noticed to be ill at ease;
Until she summised,
To her great surprise,
That her puppy was covered in fleas!

GC

A deaconess priested in **Ongar,**
Led a vicar while doing the Conga;
He tripped the fantastic,
Then grabbed her elastic,
Shouting "Can't keep it up any longer."

GRG

There was an old lady of **Orsett,**
Who rapidly took off her corset;
When it felt much too tight,
Then she saw, with a fright,
The hand of a person from Dorset.

GC

A pupil from **Paglesham Pool,**
Wore a pair of red stockings to school;
A small skirt of leather,
And a hat with a feather,
She was reckoned quite trendy and cool.

GC

There was a young girl from **Southend,**
Who drove the whole town round the bend;
Having had too much beer,
She set fire to the pier,
Behaviour that's hard to defend.

JB

There's a lady, I think, hails from **Rayne,**
Who claims a superior brain;
Through crosswords she whizzes,
Wins all the pub quizzes,
And in truth is a serious pain.

DC

A cricketing lady from **Peldon,**
Would shout out "Howzat sir! Oh well done!"
A maid from The Rose,
Said: "Well, everyone knows,
She's dropped 'em more times than she's held 'em."

GRG

The cricketing lady said

"Find me a game of great cricket,
With an oak not far from the wicket;
With pavilion and hall,
And painted church wall,
Why **Copford** will fill such a ticket."

NC

Enveloped herself in a mesh 'T';
A well-built young lady from **Pleshey,**
She had to, she said,
"I love potatoes and bread,
but they make my loose bits much too fleshy."

GC

There was a poetess from **Prittlesea,**
Named clare - but spelt with a little 'c';
When told that her rhymes,
Were erratic at times,
Said "it's 'cos I trained at the college at **Writtle**, see?"

GRG

A lady from **Quendon-with-Rickling,**
Had a most uncomfortable inkling;
That if she was able,
To see under the table,
She'd find a crude fellow, a- tickling.

GC

A lady from **Rayne** went to Spain,
But she grumbled "not ever again;
The sun burned me red,
There were fleas in my bed,
And they didn't serve drinks on the plane."

GC

In **Layer Marney** there lives a young girl,
Affectionately known as Miss Pearl;
Her cat's name is **D'Arcy,**
She's terribly classy,
We all hope she'll marry an Earl.

NC

Whilst boating one day down **The Ching,**
Fat Sue took a deep breath to sing;
But her melodious sound,
Was utterly drowned,
By her bra strap going off with a PING!

GC

A lady from snug **Shellow Bowels,**
Speaks nicely, with well-pronounced vowels;
But when moonlight glows,
She grows hair on her toes,
And chills the night air with loud howls.

GC

A lady from deep **Rotten End,**
Had a leg with a right angled bend;
It was awkward for hiking,
And worse still for biking,
But her purse she could always defend.

For this lady from far **Rotten End,**
Was unlikely her money to spend;
If asked for a loan,
She'd say, with sharp tone,
"tis wrong, both to borrow, or lend."

JC

Said a queasy young girl from **St Lawrence,**
"A life on the coast's an abhorrence;
When I sail out to sea,
I'm as sick as can be,
Not in dribs, not in drabs, but in torrents."

GC

A lady from **South Woodham Ferrers,**
Was full of irrational terrors;
The hum of a bee,
Or a fart from a flea,
Would beset her with terrible tremors.

GC

A scatty young girl from T**he Crouch,**
Lay flat on the nut doctor's couch;
"What's Up?" said the shrink,
"I'm a Joey I think,
And I live in a Kangaroo's pouch."

ME

Some girls living in **Theydon Bois,**
Like dancing late evenings with boys;
But in **Hatfield Broad Oak,**
They think it no joke,
As they're terribly sensitive to noise.

GC

He cried: "Flee with me! We'll elope!
Dear maiden from **Stanford-le-Hope!"**
- Now he impatiently waits,
While she packs cases and crates,
And lowers them down with a rope.

GC

A lady who lived by **The Twizzle,**
Said: "drat this permanent drizzle;
I think it unfair,
When I straighten my hair,
That the rain turns it back to a frizzle."

but

A damsel from **Salcott-cum-Virley,**
Had hair that was naturally curly;
And what makes this verse better,
She looked good in a sweater,
And her parents had christened her Shirley.

GC

A dancer by name of Karina,
Met a sailor from **Bradwell Marina;**
She taught him to tango,
And even fandango,
When, in fact, she was a great ballerina.

GRG

They sent, as a bit of a joke,
A shy girl from **Hatfield Broad Oak;**
To market, to buy,
An elephant's eye,
And a bag with a pig in a poke.

GC

A little old girl from **The Naze,**
Invented a wonderful craze;
She'd travel by car,
Wearing only a bra,
And quoting Shakespearean plays.

CC

There was a young teacher from **Barking**
Who was fed up to the back teeth with marking;
So she jumped in the pool,
At her secondary school,
But found, to her horror, a shark in.

PC

A female from **Tilbury** named Trish,
Ate nothing but shrimps and raw fish;
On the rocks near the docks,
She combed out her locks,
Whilst giving her tail a great swish.

Her sister, a mermaid named Grace,
Rubbed seaweed oils into her face;
Although she was dishy,
Men smelt something fishy,
And never went round to her plaice.

DF

A lady from **Layer de la Haye,**
Went fishing for salmon one day;
She thought it more fun,
To try with a gun,
So fish pie was served –Take Away!

GC

Whenever Sal wanted to doze
She'd hang from a beam by her toes;
The reason for that,
Is her Dad was a bat,
(though her Mum was from **Beaumont-cum-Moze).**

GC

A school girl from **Tolleshunt Knights,**
Liked giving the other girls frights;
She laughed at the squeals,
When they found eels in the heels,
And crabs in the toes of their tights.

GC

From **Hornchurch** came author Jilly Cooper,
Her books are really quite super;
Her real love, of course, is
To write about horses,
Polo, Riders and Rivals, super duper!

DF

An old lady said: **"Twitty Fee**
Is the daintiest of places for tea;
Tho' the scones are much longer
In smart '**Chipping Ongar,**
Whilst others like whelks, at **Creeksea**."

GC

A lady from **Twizzlefoot Bridge,**
Sat numbing her bum in a fridge;
When they said to her: "why?"
She replied, with a sigh,
"I've been stung in the stern by a midge."

GC

An undergraduate girl from **Ulting,**
Thought her third class degree most insulting;
She joined the dole queue,
Saying what she would do,
Was get a job Business Consulting.

JH-W

A shrimp girl who fished round **Wick Isles,**
Rowed her boat - whilst standing - for miles;
If she sat on the thwarts,
She'd give agonized snorts,
As she suffered severely from piles.

GC

A woman from **Chignal St James,**
Called the Bishop of **Chelmsford** rude names;
He took a swing with his crook end,
Then retreated to **Hook End**,
And told her to jump in the Thames.

GRG

An uncouth young woman from **Writtle**,
At parties the entrées did spittle;
Her neighbours she'd soak,
Whenever she spoke,
Did she care? Not a jot nor a tittle.

GC

A plump little piggy from **Wix**,
Built a cosy, warm sty out of sticks;
Then a wolf came along,
With a smile and a song,
'twere better she'd built it from bricks.

But

A piggy from **Wicken Bonhunt**,
Was born as a tiny wee runt;
To make her feel big,
This little old pig,
Developed a booming great grunt.

GC

A charming young girl of **Great Totham,**
Had a shapely and beautiful bottom;
When she took off her drawers,
There was riotous applause,
They were all very pleased she'd felt hot in 'em.

GC

A **Harwich** lass, name of Bianca,
Lit a fag on the deck of a tanker;
One leg of her drawers,
Landed in the Azores,
While her brassiere flew over Sri Lanka.

GRG

Young Evie who lived out at **Chappel,**
Tried to tempt a young man with an apple;
She'd an Egremont Russet
Concealed in her gusset,
But Adam said, "Eve, I won't grapple."

GRG

When visiting **Layer Marney Tower**,
Girls would frequently wait for an hour;
But with Nick's smart new looks,
It's all P's and no queues,
So they no longer need such staying power.

GRG

A colour-blind girl, ancient queen,
Wore red knickers that never were seen;
Until on **Downham** Road,
They washed off her woad,
And a chap said: "so that's **Wyatts Green**!"

GRG

Our Sharon went on a blind date,
With a chap who'd a chimp in a crate;
While they sat 'neath a tree,
The chimp poured them tea,
And proffered small cakes on a plate.

GC

There was a young girl from **Tiptree,**
Who was constantly playing her Wii;
She reached the next level,
And killed the Red Devil,
Not bad when bought on QVC!

But this same young girl from Tiptree,
While continuing to play on her Wii;
In the midst of a game,
Her legs went all lame,
And she landed quite hard on her knee.

VI

Sporting Sue from **Layer de la Haye,**
Spent her life watching Match of the Day;
Said her coach, "You're a loafer,
Get up off the sofa,
You've no idea of the meaning of play!"

JH-W

A mermaid who lived up the **Colne,**
Weighed nothing, just all scales and bone;
But her rotund young daughter,
Who swam the **Blackwater,**
Tipped her scales at 24 Stone.

GRG

Two old ladies, called Mavis and Sue,
Were embarrassed **at Colchester** zoo;
When a monkey they spied,
Exposed it's backside,
All mottled in purple and blue.

Meanwhile

Two bears, in the **Colchester** zoo
Were 'at it', in full public view.
'Stop'em', Sue said,
'Give 'em buns, or some bread.'
'Stop for buns!' said the Keeper. 'Would you?

GC